Copyright

You Can Publish: The Master Manual

Nina Motivates LLC

www.ninaaddison.com

publishernina@gmail.com

Graphics and Marketing: 727 Solutions

727solutionist.com

Copyright© 2025, Nina Motivates LLC

All rights reserved Nina Motivates LLC

ISBN: 979-8-9910982-4-3

Table of Contents

Introduction

Anyone can publish a book! However, when publishing, you want your book to stand out. You want your book to make an impact. You want your book to be done correctly! This manual takes away the fear of not knowing what to do or what steps to take while publishing. It is your one stop shop to write and publish your book.

The first question I always get is "how do I get started?" My response is always the same. **JUST WRITE!** We often make starting more difficult than it has to be. You may be someone who needs an outline before you get started with chapters. Or you may be a person who just needs to write everything down, then go back and organize it later. Oh, you also do not need a title to get started writing your book. A title will come as you write if you do not have one in the beginning. Trust the process.

As you go through this manual, allow yourself to go at your own pace. BUT do not allow yourself to go so slow you never get it done. Once you get started, create a daily habit of spending at least 10 minutes a day writing and working on your book. Set an appointed writing time in your daily schedule, and before you know it, you would have birthed a book! Now, let's dive in!

Step-By-Step (From your thought to your bookshelf)

Let's make a complete list before we go any further. This helps you to know what's ahead. This helps you to plan. This helps you to organize. This helps you to check off your to-do list. This also helps you not to get overwhelmed. We will go through each of these things and more as we dive further into the manual.

Step 1 – Decide to become an author.

Step 2 – Decide what you want to write about.

Step 3 – Begin writing.

Step 4 – Create a release plan.

Step 5 – Hire an editor and graphic designer (illustrator for children's books).

Step 6 – Obtain an ISBN and Barcode.

Step 7 – Format your book.

Step 8 – Start Pre-sales.

Step 9 – Market your book.

Step 10 – Upload to printing source.

Step 11 – Order a trial copy of your book before you order a bulk of books.

Step 12 – Launch your book.

Step 13 – Now Copyright!

Step 14 – Keep the momentum going!

Getting Started

The first step to writing a book is to have an idea of what you desire to write about. Some people want to write a book but have absolutely no idea what they want to write about. There are several things you could write about.

1. Your life testimony/story.

2. Something you know how to do well.

3. Something you are passionate about.

4. Something you want everyone else to know.

5. A story you have been creating in your head.

6. A Children's book.

7. A book of poetry.

8. Motivational quotes.

9. Inspirational stories.

10. D.I.Y Projects.

And the list goes on...

If you know what you want to write about, you can then begin your research. Research what has already been published about your topic. What has been popular. Research your audience. What are they in need of. How can you help them? Knowing what has been written and what your audience needs helps you to know how to deliver it in your own way.

Speaking of audience, let's touch on that subject. Your audience is who you are writing to and for. Your audience is the people who will benefit from your book the most. Many people like to say everyone, when in fact nothing is for "everyone." Although many people can benefit from your work, you want to identify a specific group of people that you are targeting. This is important for several reasons. Let's just name two…

1. It helps you to know the type of language you should use. You do not want to use big words in a baby book, if you get what I mean…

2. It helps you to know what groups to aim at when promoting your book as well.

Authors are problem solvers. When you publish a book, you are solving a problem. Even if your book is pure entertainment, it is giving someone what they need in that moment. Here is a list of questions to help you get started on your publishing journey.

1. What question would your book answer?

2. What problem would your book solve?

3. Who would your book help?

4. What impact do you want your book to make?

5. Where is your book needed?

These questions will not only give you some guidance, but it should also spark an excitement to write because it will help you see that someone is waiting for your book to enter their hands. Remove the thought that no one wants to read what you have to say. Yes, they do! Many people are waiting on your book to help them get to their next. Let go of that stinking thinking right now! Negative thoughts/self-doubt is the second reason, behind not knowing how to start, that people do not right their books. Well, we are removing all excuses.

Now that you have answered the questions, have a topic, and have begun research on what others have written about, it is time to brainstorm ideas that you want to include in your book. You may have seen some things in your research that you want to include in your book.

Remember not to take the words of others unless you are going to cite them in your work. You may have some of the same ideas and thoughts, but please do not copy them or they may bring you up on plagiarism. That is the purpose of getting your book protected with copyrights, which we will discuss later.

Some people like to make outlines, so they stay on target. Some people like to just write. Either way, do what works best for you. You do not have to do what everyone else does. You must do what is best for you. You want to get it done. Trying to do what works for everyone else may keep you from finishing your book. Your stamp on the world matters! So if you need an outline, here are some things to include in your outline: introduction, chapter title ideas, main points, conclusion points. We will discuss components of a book in the next chapter.

If you are someone who just wants to write. WRITE! Get it all out on paper. Then go back and organize. That is why you have drafts. 1st draft, 2nd draft, and a 3rd draft if needed. You do not have to have it all in order in the beginning. I have done both. For this manual, I have an outline. For books where I motivate, I just motivate. Find your grove and rock it out!

Workbook Part 1

This is to help you draft some writing ideas...

I want to write about _____

_____

_____.

I want to write about this because _____

_____

_____

_____

_____.

Remember to research your topic.

My audience is (include sex, race if applicable, age range, income bracket, where they live, etc. Include as many details as you can think of. This is your client profile/avatar.

_____

_____

_____

_____

_____

_____

_____

_____

_____.

Problem solve:

1. What question would your book answer?

_____

_____

_____

2. What problem would your book solve?

_____

_____

_____

3. Who would your book help?

_____

_____

_____

4. What impact do you want your book to make?

_____

_____

_____

5. Where is your book needed?

_____

_____

_____

The Cost of Publishing and Some Tips

The price to publish a book can vary. There is a way to publish with little to no money. Then, it can get pricy. Either way, do what is best for you. I will teach you both ways in this book. You can go on KDP (Amazon) and use their ISBN, Barcode, Book cover template, etc. and publish for free. But you want to own all your own things if possible. If you want all rights and ownership to your book, I highly recommend you pay for certain things. Let's get right into it.

ISBN is like your book's social security number. It identifies your book to you and your title. The barcode is attached to your ISBN, and it is like your social security card. It can have your price on there if you decide to put a price on it. There are times when people do not want a price, but it is helpful when your book is in different stores.

Recommended place to get your ISBN, Barcode, and Copyrights done is Bowker www.myidentifiers.com

ISBN $125

Barcode $25

Copyright $89.95

You also want to invest in a good editor. Know what you need in an editor. Yes, there are different types of editors. You have editors that only check punctuation and sentence structure. You have editors that help with typesetting/formatting, chapter title suggestions etc. You have editors that help make your book make sense. Know what you need and hire accordingly. Editing can be priced per page, or some editors have an hourly rate. It can get expensive. Do not get discouraged. Yes, you can try Grammarly 1st, that may make the cost of editing cheaper. The least I have paid for editing is $4 per page.

The next investment you want to make is in your book cover. Know what you want. Look at some styles you like. Examine what it is about the cover that got your interest. You want to be able to share these details and even pictures of the cover with the designer you choose. Please do your best to have an idea of what you like and want. Have a vision. This gives the designer something to go from when creating your cover. Know what colors fit your book. Know the style of font you like, pictures you may want etc. Covers can range from $100 and up, depending on the designer. When uploading your cover to different sites, you will need a PDF file of it. The designer will need the dimensions for the cover. This is usually gotten once you know how many pages your book is as well as the size.

What I normally do is ask them to create a JPEG of it and if they could do a sample until you know the exact dimensions of the book. Once you know the dimensions you can get your PDF copy. You can go to most printing sites and get the cover creator dimensions. This helps the designer be more accurate with the PDF copy of your cover.

If doing a children's book, you will need an illustrator. Prices vary and can get expensive depending on your desired drawings. Illustrations can be from $25 and up.

You may also decide to hire someone to do fancy formatting for you. Basic formatting is easy. But when you want more, invest.

Overall, I recommend having at least $600-$1,000 to complete your book. Up to $1,000 more if doing a children's book. You absolutely can spend less. And you do not need it all at once. Editing is going to be your biggest cost for traditional books.

Components of A Book

There are some books must haves and some optional components.

Title – What is your book about? Your title should grab the attention of your target audience. Your title should also reflect what you are writing about inside of the book.

Cover Design – Your cover should scream "buy me" to your target audience. Colors matter. Make sure your color choices match the feel you want to give your audience. Images matter. Every aspect of your cover matters. Look at some covers that interest you to get some ideas.

Copyright page – This is very important. A sample copyright page will be in a later chapter, along with how to officially copyright your work.

Signature page – This is optional. This is a page where you can sign to those who support you.

Forward page – This is optional. A forward is often written by someone you know who a credible resource is.

Acknowledgements – This is optional. Acknowledgement is the opportunity for you to thank people who have had an impact on you. It could be in general or during your process of writing the book.

Dedication – This is optional. Who are you writing the book in honor of? Many people choose a loved one or a group of people. It is also optional to say why you are dedicating it to who you are dedicating it to.

Table of Content - A page in the front of your book that lists the chapters or sections of the book and the page numbers they begin on.

Introduction – Start strong, finish strong! The introduction is your strong start. It introduces the book. It sets the stage for what the book is about. I like to think of it as the first letter from the author. Draw them in. Make the audience want to read until the last word. This is like your "one chance" to capture their attention. You want to start with a story, problem statement, or questions. You want your introduction to paint a picture.

About Author/Contact – In my opinion, every book should have information about who the author is and how the author could be contacted. Sample bio questions and a bio is included later in the manual.

Words on the back – I never leave the back of my books blank. Why? Because the cover, including the words on the cover will draw people in. What you say on the back of your book is going to possibly be the next thing a person reads after the title. And they will look at your picture if you have one on the back. Sometimes people have a few reviews. Or you can give a few power packed sentence that makes your audience say "I need this book today!"

Know Your Genre

Knowing the genre of your book is important for several reasons. It lets you know the language you need to write your book in. If it is for children, you need to write to their understanding, so on and so on. Because there are about 80 different genres, I will explain how to find your genre. When uploading your book to any print platform, you are often asked the category and sub-category of your book. You know this based off your genre. It makes filling this portion out so easy.

The easiest way to find out what your genre is, is to go to google and type in "what genre is a book that focus on…"

Genres are determined by need and audience expectation. I will list some of the most popular genres, but they are not limited to these.

Fiction Genres

Adventure: Focuses on action-packed journeys, exploration, and daring exploits. Often features a protagonist overcoming challenges in dangerous or exotic settings.

Fantasy: Features extraordinary adventures.

Science Fiction (Sci-Fi): Explores futuristic settings, advanced technology, space exploration, and speculative science.

Mystery: Focuses on solving a crime or unraveling secrets, often with a detective or amateur sleuth as the protagonist.

Romance: Centers on love stories with emotional and heartfelt themes, often culminating in a happy ending.

Thriller: Known for suspense, tension, and high stakes plots that keep readers on edge.

Historical Fiction: Set in the past, blending historical events with fictional elements.

Horror: Designed to evoke fear, often featuring supernatural elements, monsters, or psychological suspense.

Non-Fiction Genres

Biography/Autobiography: Chronicles the life of a real person, often providing insights into their achievements and struggles.

Memoir: A personal account of specific experiences or periods in the author's life.

Self-Help: Guides readers toward personal development, offering advice and strategies for improvement.

Spirituality/Religion: Explores faith, spiritual practices, and theological perspectives.

History: Explores historical events, figures, and contexts with a focus on factual accuracy.

True Crime: Examines real-life crimes and criminal investigations, often with psychological analysis.

Travel: Focuses on exploring destinations, cultures, and experiences around the world.

Science: Focuses on scientific discoveries, theories, or real-world applications, often written for general audiences.

Cookbooks: Provides recipes and culinary techniques, often with anecdotes or cultural insights.

Example: The Joy of Cooking by Irma S. Rombauer.

Personal Development: Focuses on mindset, productivity, or achieving goals.

Strategy Session – Let's Plan

A plan without a strategy is just an idea. You must add a plan to your publishing goals. Begin with the end in mind. Below is a graph I use to help me plan the release of my books and my clients. I will explain how to effectively choose dates based off the end result you desire. There is also a sample included.

Task	By	Completed On
Release Date		
Draft of Manuscript for editing		
Editing complete		
Cover complete		
Formatting complete		
Trial Copy Ordered By		
Bulk Book Ordered By		
Complete Book Release Event Planning		
Illustrations (Children Books)		

Release Date – Plan this first. When you have the goal date in mind, you can then plan everything else.

Draft of Manuscript – This is the draft you want to send to the editor. Meaning, all chapters have been written and you have gone over them several times. You should be the first, second, and third set of eyes on your work. Then the editor. Then you again. This is the first thing that would need to be completed. Ideally 3-6 months before your release date. Can it be a shorter period, like 30-60 days? Absolutely! However, take into consideration the time your editor may need to complete your edits.

Editing – You want to give an editor at least 30 days. If your book is hundreds of pages, maybe even longer. You want a professional eye on your work, even if you are a professional. A doctor usually doesn't deliver their own babies, if you know what I mean. Four eyes are better than two.

Let me make this disclaimer…. Editors miss things too. They should not miss a whole lot, but they are human too. You should get what you pay for, and if you see a bunch of mistakes they made, reach out to them.

Cover Completion – We have a whole chapter discussing your cover so let me say this, do not rush your designer. Give them at least 2-3 weeks to design. Give them all they need in a timely fashion so you do not run out of time. Your cover helps the promoting process.

Formatting/Typesetting – This is the last step before you upload your book to any print site. Give yourself two good weeks to format. You may be able to do it in a day. But you want to do it right. We will discuss this more in a later chapter.

Trail Copy – A trial copy is the copy before the bulk order. You want to see what your book looks like before you order a lot of books. You want to see what it will look like, feel like, and catch anything you may have missed. Hopefully you have no more changes needed, but don't you want to be 100% sure?

Bulk Book Order – This is the order you place that includes any pre-sales you may have got as well as books for your launch and to have on hand. Keep books on hand.

Book Release Planned/Marketing – People need to know you have a book coming out! You want people to anticipate buying your book. You also want people to come to support your launch. Throughout the entire process some form of marketing will be important. If you are going to do a live or virtual launch, you want to plan while your book is being edited.

Illustrations – This is for children's books. Depending on how detailed you desire your drawings to be, the illustrator may need a few months to draw your illustrations. There are times you can send them drawings per page or chapter, so they are not waiting on the entire manuscript. (I even do this with my book for editing). Give them time to perfect your drawings. Start with them early so they can begin drafting samples for you.

When you get ready to submit all documents to the graphic designer for your cover, you want to purchase your ISBN and barcode and download the PDF of the barcode to send to your designer for the back of your book cover.

Sample

Task	By	Completed On
Release Date	6/1/25	
Draft of Manuscript for editing	3/1/25	
Editing complete	4/1/25	
Cover complete	3/1/25	
Formatting complete	4/20/25	
Trial Copy Ordered By	4/25/25	
Bulk Book Ordered By	5/10/25	
Complete Book Release Event Planning	4/15/25	
Illustrations (Children Books)	4/15/25	

Writing Plan

Set time daily to write and document it! It is just that simple. You want to get your book done? Take time daily to write. 10 minutes a day minimum! Start with ten. You have ten minutes to spare, trust me! That 10 minutes may turn into 30 minutes or even an hour. The main point is to start somewhere! Below is your time tracker. Document how much time you spend a day writing. Then celebrate each time you write. You can reward yourself with a TV show, or a special treat.

Date/Day of the week	Time start writing	Time complete	Total time spent

Date/Day of the week	Time start writing	Time complete	Total time spent

Date/Day of the week	Time start writing	Time complete	Total time spent

Date/Day of the week	Time start writing	Time complete	Total time spent

Date/Day of the week	Time start writing	Time complete	Total time spent

Date/Day of the week	Time start writing	Time complete	Total time spent

Date/Day of the week	Time start writing	Time complete	Total time spent

Date/Day of the week	Time start writing	Time complete	Total time spent

Date/Day of the week	Time start writing	Time complete	Total time spent

Date/Day of the week	Time start writing	Time complete	Total time spent

Date/Day of the week	Time start writing	Time complete	Total time spent

Book Covers & Illustrations

The first thing people see before reading a word in your book is your book cover! Everything about your book cover matters. The colors, the title, the name, EVERY SINGLE THING!

Colors have meaning. Colors put people in a certain mood. If you pick up a book that has dark tones, you may think it is a sad or scary book. If you pick up a book with bright colors, you will think more happy thoughts. There is actually a psychology to picking the colors for your book cover.

Red: Red is frequently associated with danger, violence, and passion.

Blue: Blue is often seen as calming, serene, and trustworthy.

Yellow: Yellow is consistently associated with happiness, optimism, and sunshine.

Orange: Orange often suggests excitement.

Green: Green is associated with nature and peace.

Purple: Purple is a luxurious color that represents royalty and prestige.

Pink: Pink is often used on book covers to evoke emotions such as romance, love, and happiness.

Brown: Brown is often correlated with the color of earth and can imply stability.

Black: The color black is often used on book covers to evoke a sense of mystery, suspense, or danger.

Let's put this to the test! Go grab a few books from your bookshelf and look at the colors and the titles. Do the book color choices follow this phycology? When you are choosing your colors for your cover, know the goal of your book. You want to grab your audience's attention in the beginning.

The font and style of your title matters as well. Here are my three top recommendations when choosing the font and style for your cover. 1. What will appeal to your audience? 2. Is it legible? 3. Be creative, but within reason!

Who is your book for? If your book is for children, you may use bigger bolder fonts that will grab the child's attention. Maybe for senior citizens as well because they look for easy to read books. If you are writing a romance novel, you may use more fancy style and a medium size font. Once again, my suggestion is to look up some books in your genre and get a few ideas. But you want to stand apart.

Make sure your title font and style are legible. You do not want to run people off because they cannot figure out what the title is. Yes, be creative, but within reason. Some fonts are not meant for book covers.

You want to be creative. You want your title to stand out. You want to be innovative as much as possible. Make your audience pick up your book and desire not to put it down.

When working on your cover, or working with a designer for your cover, please be sure not to forget the spine or back of book. Let's quickly talk about the spine. If your book is small, less than 100 pages, many printing places prefer no words on your spine. This is because it will either be too small to be seen or there is no room for it.

Your back cover is very important. It is the first thing people see. Every detail about it is important. To get the dimensions of your cover for upload you can go to your print site and/or go to google and type in "book cover calculator for (inset printing site)." Then you will put in information about the size of the book, the page numbers and a few other details. They will then give you the size you can send to your graphic designer as well as a template depending on your printing source.

You want your cover in both JPEG and PDF and you want a copy of just the front cover if you decide to upload your book as an eBook.

Illustrations – Illustrations are often used in children's books and sometimes in books where a picture can enhance a point. Illustrations are pictures that bring your writing to life.

Illustrators need to know your vision. Know what type of styles you like. Look through past illustrations of things that caught your eye. Get a sample drawing from the illustrator to be sure they are perfect for you. Give them examples of illustrations you like. Have a vision. Be clear with the illustrator. The more information you give them, the better they can be with your illustrations.

Workbook Part 2

What should my cover say to my audience?

_____

_____

_____

Colors for My Book cover and why...

_____

_____

_____

Will I use images and why...

_____

_____

_____

Words for the back of my book...

_____

_____

_____

_____

_____

_____

_____

_____

_____

_____

Copyright

After you've approved your work, you want to get it copyrighted to protect your work. I always wait until my work is complete before I copyright because I want to be sure I have made all changes that are needed. There are two ways you can copyright. You can do your ISBN, your Barcode, and your Copyright all from the same website... **www.myidentifiers.com** (my preferred one stop shop)

Or you could go to

https://www.copyright.gov (here are their steps)

1.   Go to the Copyright.gov portal

2.   On the left box, select "Literary Works"

3.   Navigate to "Register a Literary Work" on the right sidebar

4.   Select either "new user" or login with your account

5.   If you're a new user, fill out your information

6.   Navigate to "Copyright Registration" on the left and select "Register A New Claim"

7.   Select "Start Registration"

8.   Fill out the copyright form

9.   Pay your $85 copyright fee to complete registration

10.   Submit your finished manuscript to the U.S. Copyright Office

Copyright Page Sample

Copyright

Book title

Anointed Hands Publishing

Nina Addison (Nina Motivates)

www.ninamotivates.info

publishernina@gmail.com

Graphics and Marketing: Name and Information

Editor: Name and Information

ISBN: 978-1-0000000-0-0

Write Your Book!

A book is not a book until you write it! You want to make sure your book is consistent with content and that it discusses only what it is intended to discuss. You can write multiple books. So, stay focus on the current task at hand.

Your book will have an introduction, body (the chapters), and conclusion (the last chapter). Just like we learned in school, your book will have a flow. You want your book to start strong. Your introduction will grab your audience and make them want to keep reading.

Let's talk about the introduction, then we will break it down step-by-step. Start your introduction with a strong hook. This could be a dramatic experience that people could visualize. You could also use a quote, scripture, statistic, question or bold statement. The introduction is where you could address your audience. You also want to state the purpose of the book. Let them know what they will learn or gain from reading your book. You are the expert. This is your chance to gain credibility.

Connect to your audience emotions. We are emotional readers. We want you to touch us where we are drawn into your story. Often people write their introductions last. Why? Well because after you have poured out, you know how to introduce all you have given.

Develop Your Concept

- **Identify Your Purpose**: Decide what you want your book to achieve—educate, entertain, inspire, or instruct.

- **Define Your Audience**: Understand who your readers are and what they want from your book.

- **Outline Your Core Idea**: Summarize your book's main message or story in one or two sentences to keep your focus clear.

Create an Outline or Draft Ideas (This step is for those who need an outline. If you are someone who likes to write then organize, that is fine. There is more than one right way!)

- Break your manuscript into chapters or sections.

- Draft the main points, scenes, or topics for each chapter.

- Organize the flow logically—e.g., chronological for a memoir, or problem-solution for non-fiction.

Write a First Draft

> ➢ Don't Aim for Perfection: Focus on getting ideas onto the page without worrying too much about grammar or phrasing.

Complete Your First Review

- **Edit for Content**: Ensure your ideas are clear, the structure makes sense, and the pacing works.

- **Enhance Your Language**: Refine your word choice, sentence structure, and tone to match your audience and genre.

- **Seek Feedback**: Share your draft with trusted peers, beta readers, or writing groups for constructive criticism.

Professional Editing – Hire Someone! Check the Resource Chapter

- **Developmental Editing**: Focuses on big-picture issues like structure, plot, and character development.

- **Line Editing**: Polishes the language and flow at the paragraph and sentence level.

- **Copyediting and Proofreading**: Catches grammar, punctuation, spelling, and formatting errors.

At the end of this book, there are pages to get you to write! If you feel inspired now, put a bookmark here and turn to the back and write away!

Visit my YouTube for quick videos on writing your manuscript and more.

www.youtube.com/ninamotivates

Editing

Editing is a very important step in the publishing process. I will provide some recommendations for editors in the resource chapter. I highly recommend you hire a professional editor. Even if you are a great editor, it is good to have another set of eyes on your work.

Before you send to an editor do the following. This could cut down your editing costs drastically.

- ✓ Re-read your book. Books should sound like you but be grammatically correct. Often people write books how they talk, but that is not always correct grammar.

- ✓ Spell words out. We live in a shorthand spelling world, but in books words should be spelled out.

- ✓ Make sure you understand your sentences.

- ✓ Make sure paragraphs flow.

- ✓ Make sure you have titled each chapter.

- ✓ Make sure the titles make sense to the chapters.

- ✓ Check for punctuation.

- ✓ Do a final read-through to catch any remaining issues.

- ✓ Use tools like Grammarly or ProWritingAid for additional checks.

Formatting

I prefer to format my book in Microsoft word unless I am doing a children's book, workbook or something with colors. You have so many options. I will give a few. I am going to start with what I know, Microsoft word.

Formatting made easy in word

• 6x9 Traditional book size (choose the size that works for you)

• 8.5x11 Class books, workbooks, etc.

• 4x7 or smaller size Devotionals, pocket size

• In word document, go to layout, page setup, paper then adjust the width and height (example 6W 9H traditional book size)

• Margin 1" all around, Orientation Portrait, Layout – apply to whole document

• Want to be consistent with font throughout document for some printing sources

Check the requirements needed for the printing/publishing source you choose. All printers are not the same.

Steps to formatting

Page Size: Set your page dimensions to 6x9 inches.

In Microsoft Word: Go to Layout > Size > More Paper Sizes and input 6 inches (width) and 9 inches (height).

In Google Docs: Go to File > Page Setup and set custom page dimensions.

Margins: Set 1-inch margins on all sides.

In Word: Go to Layout > Margins > Custom Margins and input 1 inch for Top, Bottom, Left, and Right.

Be sure to Choose a Readable Font and Size

Use clean, professional fonts like Garamond, Times New Roman, Georgia, or Palatino for the body text.

Font size: Use 11 or 12 pt for the main text.

Avoid decorative or overly fancy fonts for body text to maintain readability.

Set Paragraph Styles

Alignment: Justify the text for a clean and professional appearance.

Line Spacing: Use 1.15 or 1.5 spacing for readability.

Indentation: Indent the first line of each paragraph by 0.25 or 0.5 inches (not a tab or extra spaces).

In Word: Adjust this in Paragraph > Indents and Spacing.

Avoid extra spaces between paragraphs unless you're switching sections.

Add Headers and Footers

Headers: Include the book title on the left page (even pages) and the author's name or chapter title on the right page (odd pages).

Footers: Add page numbers, typically centered at the bottom or aligned with the right margin.

Leave headers/footers off the first page of each chapter (this is called a "drop header").

Format Chapter Titles

Use a larger font size (e.g., 14-16 pt) for chapter titles.

Center align chapter titles and leave a blank space before starting the chapter text.

Consider using bold or small caps for titles to make them stand out.

Start each chapter on a new page.

Maintain Consistency

Use consistent fonts, sizes, and spacing throughout the book.

Check that headings, subheadings, and other design elements are formatted uniformly.

Insert Section Breaks or Page Breaks

Use section breaks for major divisions, such as between chapters.

In Word: Go to Layout > Breaks > Section Breaks > Next Page to start a new chapter or section.

Use "Print Preview" to verify layout consistency.

Save and Export

Save your document in its original format (e.g., DOCX).

Export to PDF for print-ready formatting, as most printing platforms like Amazon KDP or IngramSpark require PDF files.

ALWAYS EMAIL YOURSELF A COPY OF YOUR UPDATED WORK WHEN YOU WORK ON IT!

Tools to Consider:

Microsoft Word or Google Docs: Great for basic formatting.

Scrivener: Excellent for managing and organizing long manuscripts.

Adobe InDesign: Best for advanced formatting and design.

Vellum (Mac users): Simplifies book formatting for print and eBooks.

Embed your fonts!

To embed fonts in a document, you can do the following:

1. Open the document

2. Select the File tab

3. Select Options (bottom lefthand corner)

4. Select the Save tab

5. Under Preserve fidelity when sharing this document, check the Embed fonts in the file box

6. Click OK

You can also embed fonts in PDFs using PDF editors.

Embedding fonts in PDFs

- You can embed fonts in PDFs using Word

- You can use PDF editors like PDF-XChange Editor, SmallPDF, or iLovePDF

- You can choose to embed all fonts

Printing Resources

There are many sites you could use to print your book. Here are a few suggestions. Information was taken directly from their website.

IngramSpark - https://www.ingramspark.com *(#1 Recommendation)*

- ✓ Global distribution to over 45,000 retailers & libraries

- ✓ Availability to Amazon, Apple, Kobo, and Barnes & Noble

- ✓ Print quality and e-reader compatibility

- ✓ Online sales reporting

- ✓ All managed from a single platform

- ✓ Free to use

KDP (Amazon) - kdp.amazon.com

- ✓ Self-publish easily

- ✓ Publish print and digital formats in three simple steps, and see your book appear on Amazon stores around the world in 72 hours.

- ✓ Earn more

- ✓ Earn up to 70% royalty and offer your eBook on Kindle Unlimited by enrolling in KDP Select

- ✓ Keep control

- ✓ Retain ownership of your content, publish on your schedule, and set your own list prices.

Lulu - www.lulu.com

- ✓ Publish or Print a Book - Have a book custom printed or self-publish a book for free to sell around the world!

- ✓ Free resources & tools to get you started with Self-Publishing and Print-On-Demand books.

- ✓ Sell your books internationally using Shopify, WooCommerce, Amazon, the Lulu Bookstore, and more.

- ✓ Connect your business site with Lulu's free book printing API. Have copies professionally printed and shipped automatically.

The Book Patch – www.thebookpatch.com

I have not used them in years. When I first started publishing, they were my go-to. It was easy and affordable for me and my clients. I honestly need to try them again. I do see their website is updated, so I am sure they have updated their services.

48 Hour Books – www.48hourbooks.com

My emergency printing source. If you need books within a week, 48 Hour is the go-to. Yes, books are more expensive, but the quality is amazing!

Pricing Your Book

There are things you want to consider when deciding the price of your book. You do not want to lose money nor just break even. Books are a source of income for many. You want to first know the approximate amount it would cost to print your book. Each printing site has a price calculator so you can know how much it costs to print them.

Books used to cost $10. Now books go for $20 or more. You want to at least double or triple your costs. The going rate to print books is $2.50-$5.00. *If you are printing a children's book or hard back book, the cost could be much more expensive.*

You also want to consider shipping. Now, if you plan to have books shipped to you then shipped to your client, you may want to go closer to the $25 price range because you will be paying double shipping. Many people want their books signed, so instead of shipping the book directly from a printing site, you would need to ship it to you first. Always have books in stock.

Additional tips on pricing your book:

1. Research the prices books in your genre and size sale for.

2. Understand your audience and their budget.

3. Leave room to give deals and sales.

Book Collaborations

Book collaborations are very popular and can be a blessing to you and those who join your collaboration. Collaborations are a great way to help people become authors without having to write an entire book. Usually, the collaborator sets the rules to join and the benefits. If you decide to put a collaboration together, here are some things to consider.

1. What will your collaboration be about and who would benefit from being an author?

2. What is the time frame for the writing and publishing of the book?

3. How many authors do you desire?

4. How will you promote and search for authors?

5. Will the authors have the opportunity to sell books at a discounted rate?

6. How will you communicate with your authors?

7. Will you provide a general community space for your authors like a Facebook group, app to connect (groupme, band, slack etc.)?

8. How much is the investment for authors?

9. How many flyers will the authors get to promote?

10. Will authors receive any books with their investment?

11. Will authors be able to obtain more books at a discounted rate after the launch?

12. Will you host a book launch virtually or in-person?

I often use goggle forms to collect data from my authors and I make charts to keep track of the things they turn in like their pictures, phone, email address, bios, payments, and entry. I am attaching pictures to show a sample of my google form.

Dear God (Adult & Youth) Collaboration Opportunity

Dear God is a 31 day devotional written in the form of letters to God.

Authors can write up to 250 words in a letter form pouring their heart out to God.

This book is created as a devotion and journal. Letters to God is a way to grow in God and help other people learn that they too can communicate with God in their own way, from the heart.

Your letter could be to praise Him, ask Him for something, worship Him, Love on him, or whatever your heart desires.

Here is the exciting news.... Two versions of this devotion will be produced. A version for 18+ and one for youth ages 8+ (a youth younger is able to contribute, contact Nina)

Only 31 youth and 31 adult spots.

Books will be released April 1, 2025.

Entry due February 15th.

Books will be released April 1, 2025.

Entry due February 15th.

Books will Pre-sale $20 (you make $10) regular price $25 (you make $15).

Cost $100 per author (youth or adult) $25 deposit required, balance due January 31st.

Funds go towards...
- Book Cover
- Formatting
- Edits
- Flyer
- Rights to sell book and co-author publishing rights

Some of the Benefits for you:
Become an author.
Sale the book at market rate and keep the royalties.
You get an author copy of the book for participating as well.

Communication will be through email publishernina@gmail.com and via text 872-213-5858

coachninamotivates@gmail.com
Switch account

Not shared

* Indicates required question

Name *

Your answer

Phone Number *

Your answer

Email Address *

Your answer

Mailing Address (For your author copy   *
of the book)

Your answer

Are you able to write a letter of up to   *
250 words and email to
publishernina@gmail.com by February
15th?

Are you willing to invest $100 towards   *
publication of the book? Only $25 due
to reserve spot, balance due by January
31st.

○ Yes

○ No

Payments can be sent via Zelle 773-   *
383-6497, Cashapp $ninamotivates, or
an invoice can be sent vis PayPal. How
do you prefer to pay?

Your answer

Is this form for a youth or adult? *

○ Youth

○ Adult

More Information
We are so excited to have you join this
amazing collaboration. You can use this
opportunity to become an author or have

More Information

We are so excited to have you join this amazing collaboration. You can use this opportunity to become an author or have another book under your arsenal of books. You will email all responding information to publishernina@gmail.com

We will also need a headshot and name as you would like it to appear in the book and on promotional materials sent to publishernina@gmail.com   You can email the above email with any questions, comments or concerns.

Once form is complete, You will get an email within 24 hours confirming you are in.

Payments can be sent via Zelle 773-38̶3̶-̶6̶4̶9̶7̶, Cashapp $ninamotivates, or an invoice can be sent vis PayPal.

Thank You!

Submit   Clear form

Google Forms

Sample Information from one of my past collaborations

Name of Book

This book is to motivate and give hope to those who are going through hard times in life. We are seeking adult authors (men and women over 18) that have gone through but have come out on the side of success! You can inspire someone through your testimony! Here is your opportunity...

You can also put a summary of a solo book in this book to give more exposure to your solo project.

Authors write up to 2,000 words

Book will be released September 2023

Book release details:

Entry due August 15th

Edits completed by September 8th

Print draft September 20th

Release September 26th

Interviews begin in August

Pre-Sales begin in August

Books will Pre-sale $20 (you make $10) regular price $25 (you make $15)

Cost $400 ($100 deposit required to secure your space and to get your promotional flyer done, Balance due by August 15th)

Funds go towards...

- Book Cover

- Formatting

- Edits

- 2 Promo flyers (author announcement and pre-sale flyer)

- Virtual interview one-on-one

- 5 Copies of Book

- Order additional books at wholesale price ($10) and sell at market rate ($25)

- Coaching through the process

- Private group for follow up and support

- Virtual Launch Party

- Contact Information listed in book

- Rights to sell book and co-author publishing rights

Children Books, Poetry Books, Devotionals, and Journals

Children's Books

Children's books are fun, but a lot of work must go into it. Children's books are colorful. Please carefully think of the colors you will use when doing a children's book. Different colors stimulate children differently. You want to look up the main colors you will use to be sure the goal of your book is achieved.

Children's books must be written appropriately for the ages they are for. When writing books for children, you want to stay within a 1–3-year bracket. A 0–1-year-old needs the most simplistic books. Parents are reading these books. To them. 2–3-year-olds are learning letters and possibly some two to three letter words. 4–5-year-olds are learning to read four and five letter words. And so on. Be mindful of your target audience. Know that some children learn to read faster than others.

Younger children like bigger letters and LOTS of pictures. You may not want to be too wordy with younger children. More pictures, less words.

Ryme, rhythm, and repetition are keys with children. That is how they learn and remember.

Hire an illustrator! You want your pictures to be professional. You want to let the pictures tell what the words say. Children learn best by imagery.

Look at children's books you like. Look at the size of the book, the language, everything about the book. We get inspiration from the work of others. Please do not identically duplicate any book. You can have the same book size and colors, but make sure you do not plagiarize anyone's work.

Publishing a children's book can be a bit more expensive than a traditional book. This is due to the color and premium paper you want to use so that your book is of high quality. It is always better to print a bulk of children books at one time. But do not forget to print your trial copy first! A successful children's book should spark imagination, create joy, and leave a lasting message.

Poetry Books

When publishing poetry books you want to have a purpose. Poetry is beautiful. When publishing a poetry book, you want it to flow as much as possible. You can put several parts in your poetry book to keep the topics the same. Here are simple steps to putting your poetry book together.

1. Know your poetry pattern of writing.

2. Choose your poems for your book.

3. Put the poems in the order you desire for them to appear in the book.

4. Separate by parts or chapters if poems vary.

5. Be creative with the font and formatting if poems are short.

You format poetry books much easier than traditional books. You may want to keep the words to the left or even in the middle. You do not have to justify poetry books. It is recommended to keep one poem per page.

Poetry books may be easier to read, but they tell a story and draw the readers in with each stanza.

Devotionals

Devotionals are fun and easier to do than full books. A devotional is short thought-provoking writings that are intended to inspire, uplift or deepen your spiritual growth. You want your devotional book to follow a central theme. You want your devotional book to be for a specific audience, just as in traditional books. Some devotionals include space to write and reflect as well. Your devotional should be personable, relatable, and interactive. Asking questions at the end of your entry helps the reader apply the days learning to their own lives. Devotionals can be 30, 60, or even 365 days. You get to choose how many days your devotional book will be. Many devotionals are also smaller in size than a traditional 6x9 book. Devotionals are good for those who want to share their faith.

Journals

Journals are one of the easiest things to publish. You can be fun and creative with journals. Canva makes doing journals easy. Journals can be general or have a theme. Having a theme makes the best journals. You can be as simple as having a scripture, quote or action step, to having full activity pages.

Journals are more personal. They almost serve as diaries of today. You want to consider your audience just as in traditional books. Engaging prompts are beneficial in journals. I encourage you to be creative with the design of your journal. Journals are very popular and help people to become instant authors without having to write a full book.

Marketing Through the Process and Beyond

Promote your book!

One way to hold yourself accountable is to TALK ABOUT YOUR BOOK! A book that no one knows about is not a book, it is a school assignment. You remember those papers we use to have to do in school, right? We wrote them, and after the teacher read and graded them, we threw them right in the garbage. Do not let your book have the same results. Talk about your book as if your next meal depended upon it. Here are steps to promote your book.

1.   Post quotes from your book on social media.

2.   Share your book cover.

3.   Ask questions that direct your audience attention to your book.

4.   Post videos/go live... **DO NOT BE SCARED**! (Scared money doesn't make money).

5.   Use what you have!

6.   Make a list of your warm market (people you know) and inform them.

7.   Hit up those you do not know, your cold market (if they say no, you will live).

8.   Promote DAILY!

9.   Get on podcasts, start a YouTube channel and find the social media outlet that works best for you.

10.   Be present! Show up!

Your book is part of you, part of your brand, and is your new baby! When something exciting happens you talk about it, post it and keep talking about it. You share, share, share. When a new child is born, you see more pictures of them than anything. Each milestone has new pictures attached to it etc. Treat your book as such!

In any way you can, invest in your book! Get promo videos done, testimonials, flyers, go live, do interviews, post it wherever and whenever you can. You see ads on social media all day. You may have even bought into some of them. Be that person that never stops talking about your book. Be that person that shares their book information daily. Be that person that is proud of what they have accomplished. YES, Be that person!

Join groups that your book relates to. Put on your own events, lives and use social media to your advantage. Inbox people. Be personable. You can do this. Create a fan page. Step out of your comfort zone and WORK IT!

Author Bio Questions and Sample

Bio Questionnaire (include a bio so people can connect with and contact you)

This information is to be taken and placed in paragraph form.

Your Full name/Name you would like on your bio

Family information (For example are you a wife/husband, mother/father etc.)

Hometown you were born in

Current City/State of residency

Educational background

Employment Highlights

Ministry Highlights

Special accomplishments/awards received

Contact information/Social media links

Other information you wish to include (future plans, hobbies, affiliations, ministry affiliations, anecdotes, life purpose, volunteer experience etc.)

Headshot - Important to have a professional headshot for the back of your book. You want people to take you seriously. It can be a fun look, just make sure it is professional.

Sample Bio

Dr. Nina M. Addison was born and raised in Chicago, IL and still resides in the Chicagoland area. Nina is a wife and full-time bonus mom to an amazing teenage boy. Nina received a BS in Human Development and Family Studies and studied for her master's in social work with a focus on Child and Family Studies.

Nina received an honorary Doctorate in Philosophy in Christian Leadership and Business. Nina also received the Presidential Lifetime Achievement Award. Nina is an author of over a dozen books and has assisted over 100 people in becoming published authors. Now, Nina teaches publishing through her self-paced digital course. Nina has received several awards for speaking and leadership.

Nina is a Youth Pastor and is the dean of a non-profit organization called Homeschool Helps. Nina motto is "my difference makes a difference" which she uses her physical "handicap" to show people they could do anything they need to do, want to do, and desire to do. With this, Nina has relaunched her inspirational speaking career "Nina Motivates" and is looking forward to returning as a traveling inspirational speaker.

"The only limits you have are the limits you put upon yourself"

You can connect with Nina via her website www.ninaaddison.com or via social media @ninamotivates

Brain Dump

Have an email address just for your books. This helps you keep up with everything in one spot.

Do not let writers block, block you

Writer's block is an EXCUSE! There could be so many reasons you are "stuck". Could it be that you need a break for a few minutes? Could it be that you are dealing with a touchy subject and need someone to talk to get over the hump? (Feel free to book a strategy session with me on my website if you need a coach for a day www.ninamotivates.com). Could it be that you need to do more research? My point is, there is a reason.

Take a moment and think any time this comes upon you. If you feel you cannot figure out why you are stuck, simply walk away and do something to motivate you. Here are some great tips to assist you with refocusing...

1.   Examine why you are stuck

2.   Go watch something funny

3.   Go call the most motivating person you know

4.   Re-read what you have already written and the write

Sometimes you have to do more than one step, but if you do the steps, it will work for you!

Here are some bonus things I want to include for you to have...

Headshot - Important to have a professional headshot for the back of your book. You want people to take you seriously. It can be a fun look, just make sure it is professional.

Becoming a Bestseller

Becoming a best seller requires strategy and often an investment. There are many ways you can become a bestseller. If this is your desire, you want to build an audience before your book is released. You want to come up with deals and research how bestsellers became best sellers.

To become an Amazon bestseller many people use their campaign method. In this method, you usually sell your book at a very low rate or gift eBooks for free for an amount of time and get as many people as possible to buy and download your book. You choose the right categories that will give you the traction you need for your genre. You, promote before the campaign day. You could also invest in a company to do your bestseller drive for you.

To be a New York bestseller, you must sell thousands of books. It is possible!

In the resource guide there is an expert in helping you become a bestseller.

"Dr. Nina I am writing about real life and real people, but I do not want to get sued, what do I do?"

First, you do not use names! Second, you put a disclaimer in your book stating that the names have been changed to protect the identity of the character. I usually put it on the copyright page. If people are willing, I have them sign a waiver. Especially if you are using pictures of people. Protect yourself from everyone! Change up some details. Tell the truth with a twist. Avoid misrepresentation. Anything that is public records can be used. But if it is not, please be mindful. Here's a sample consent form. If you cannot get their consent, avoid any pictures of them and their names.

Character Release and Consent Agreement

This Character Release and Consent Agreement ("Agreement") is made and entered into on this [Date], by and between:

1. "Releasor" (the individual giving consent):

Full Legal Name: [Releasor's Full Name]

Address: [Releasor's Address]

Phone: [Releasor's Contact Information]

Email: [Releasor's Email]

AND

"Author" (the individual using the Releasor's likeness and story):

Full Legal Name: [Author's Full Name]

Address: [Author's Address]

Phone: [Author's Contact Information]

Email: [Author's Email]

1. Grant of Rights

The Releasor hereby grants the Author the irrevocable, worldwide, and unrestricted right to use their name, likeness, personal experiences, and statements (collectively referred to as "Character Depiction") in connection with the book tentatively titled "[Book Title]" (the "Work"), including any future editions, adaptations, and related media.

2. Scope of Use

The Releasor understands that the Character Depiction may be used in:

Books (print, digital, and audiobook formats)

Promotional materials and marketing

Television, film, or other adaptations

Other media as determined by the Author

The Releasor acknowledges that the Author may alter or fictionalize elements of the Character Depiction.

3. Waiver of Legal Claims

The Releasor waives any right to sue the Author, publisher, or any third parties associated with the Work for:

Defamation (libel, slander, or misrepresentation)

Invasion of privacy (public disclosure of private facts, false light, or appropriation)

Emotional distress or reputational harm

4. No Compensation or Royalties

The Releasor acknowledges that they are not entitled to financial compensation, royalties, or any ownership rights in the Work unless otherwise agreed in a separate written contract.

5. Representations and Warranties

The Releasor represents that:

They are at least 18 years old and legally competent to sign this Agreement.

They have read and fully understand the terms of this Agreement.

They voluntarily enter into this Agreement without coercion.

6. Governing Law & Dispute Resolution

This Agreement shall be governed by the laws of [State/Country]. Any disputes shall be resolved through mediation or arbitration before pursuing legal action.

7. Entire Agreement

This Agreement constitutes the entire understanding between the parties. No amendments shall be valid unless made in writing and signed by both parties.

8. Signature & Acknowledgment

Releasor:

Name: [Releasor's Name]

Signature: _____

Date: [MM/DD/YYYY]

Author:

Name: [Author's Name]

Signature: _____

Date: [MM/DD/YYYY]

If minors are involved, a parent or legal guardian must sign on their behalf.

If possible, have the document notarized for extra legal protection.

If you are using photos of anyone besides yourself, please get permission and have them sign a document giving you permission.

Resources

727 Solutions

https://727.solutions

Editor

Dr. VMST
drvmst@gmail.com
drvmst.com

As an editor, I use Microsoft Word with track changes and the comment box to provide edits.

I provide line editing & copy editing which includes:

- Word choice
- Intended meaning
- Clarity
- Repetition
- Redundancy
- Consistency
- Grammar
- Syntax

Editing prices are $4-7 per page. The price is dependent upon how much time will need to be allocated and edits needed to be made.

Lola Ru
BOOKS & BEYOND

Skilled Coaching Programme

THE AUTHOR GLOW

"ARISE, WRITE & SHINE"

◆ PRAY & PLAN

◆ PRAISE & PRODUCE

◆ PROCLAIM & PROMOTE

◆ PROSPER & PUBLISH

MORE INFORMATION

📞 +447733649520/+263772391051

🌐 www.lolaru.co.zw

📷 @lolaruzw

The Glow Coach
LOLA RU
Bestselling and Award winning Author &
Author Coach | Therapist | Multipreneur

glow
N.O.A
Inspired Journeys

MONICA WILLIAMS "MORGAN"
PROFESSIONAL WRITING SERVICES

OUR MISSION IS TO SUPPORT CORPORATIONS & INDIVIDUALS BY DEVELOPING STRATEGIES & SOLUTIONS TO BUILD BETTER SUCCESS FROM THE INSIDE OUT

PROFESSIONAL WRITING SERVICES

- PROFESSIONAL BIOS
- PROOFREADING
- COPYWRITING SERVICES
- BOOK & DOCUMENT EDITING
- NEW HIRE MANUALS
- TRAINING MANUALS
- RESUME & COVER LETTERS
- LETTERS OF INTENT FOR PROPOSALS
- GRANT WRITING
- REQUEST FOR FUNDING PROPOSALS [RFP'S]

CREATIVE WRITING SERVICES

- MEMORIAL POEMS: HONORING THE LEGACY OF FAMILY MEMBERS
- POETRY & SPECIALIZED MESSAGES
- QUOTES FOR SPECIAL EVENTS & OCCASIONS

TESTIMONIALS

"MONICA IS A WONDERFULLY GIFTED AND TALENTED WRITER AND AUTHOR. SHE HAS THE UNIQUE TALENT OF TRANSPOSING WORDS AND PHRASES INTO A VERY UNIQUE, DYNAMIC WRITING."

~ BEVERLY BROWN CEO OF DREAMSTEERER/ CREATIVE CONSULTING DREAMS

"MONICA DID WELL IN CAPTURING THE ESSENCE OF THE STYLE AND MADE THE EDITS ALIGN."

~ KRYSTYLLE RICHARDSON — LIFE INNOVATION GLOBAL

"AFTER WORKING WITH MONICA WILLIAMS FOR TWO PROJECTS TO HELP UPDATE SOME OF OUR MARKETING MATERIALS AND BIOS FOR IN A BEIN, SHE HAS A WAY OF TAKING THE VISION AND MAKING WORDS COME TO LIFE ON PAPER. WE LOOK FORWARD TO WORKING WITH HER ON UPCOMING PROJECTS."

~MIKE LOGAN — IN A BEIN FOUNDER & CEO

CONTACT INFORMATION

PHONE: (443) 330-7791
EMAIL: CHANGETODAY4U@GMAIL.COM

POSTER BY: I AM FLY, LLC © 2023 CHANGE TODAY, LLC

INVISIBLE
DAUGHTER, LLC

- Manuscript Editing & Formatting
- Self Publishing Coaching
- Transparency Motivation
- Writing Coaching
- Ghost Writing

Mikkita Moore

PAYMENT PLANS AVAILABLE

$350

Deposit required

STANDARD

Manuscript to book editing and formatting

4- one on one book coaching sessions

Final manuscript to Book reading

Book upload walk through

Book ordering walk through

$850

PREMIUM

Manuscript to book editing and formatting

6- one on one book coaching sessions

Final manuscript to Book reading

Book upload walk through

Book ordering walk through

$1600

*Premium also includes

- Book Cover Design
- ISBN Number
- Book announcement flyer
- Book presale flyer

Contact us at
WWW.MIKKITAMOORE.COM
INFO@MIKKITAMOORE.COM

Jaidyn Funches
Email: Jaidynf7185@gmail.com
theartofjaidyn

 **Words Work**
Publishing

Turn your manuscript into a masterpiece

Your Words. Our Expertise. A Book That Sells

Giavonni Nickson Downing
Creative Director, Author

Custom Book Cover Design
Eye-catching covers that sell

Professional Interior Formatting
A seamless, reader-friendly layout

Print Formatting
Designed for Kindle, IngramSpark, and more

Book Launch Marketing
Promo graphics, mock-ups, press kits and more

You've poured your heart into your story—now let us transform it into a polished, professional masterpiece. A stunning book design and layout can make all the difference in captivating readers, increasing sales, and expanding your reach.

Ready to launch?

67

YOU
CAN PUBLISH

Write & Publish Your Book!

You Can Publish Digital Course

Self-Pace

Modules range from 5 to 20 minutes in length. You will have lifetime access to the course materials. Depending on your current progress, you can publish your work in as little as a week.

Step-By-Step Process

Haven't begun your writing journey? No problem! Have you completed your book but feel unsure about the next steps? Don't worry! The modules guide you through the process step-by-step, providing all the resources necessary to get your book published and in your hands quickly.

Templates and eBook Included

Included are ready-made templates, printable documents, and a bonus copy of the "You Can Publish Master Manual."

Dr. Nina M. Addison

Dr. Nina has been a published author for 12 years and founded her own publishing company 9 years ago. Her impressive accomplishments include:

- Helping over 100 individuals achieve their goal of becoming published authors.

- 3 years of experience in teaching publishing.

- Recognized as a bestselling author.

- Collaborating on 10 different books.

You Have the Power to Publish!

This course allows you to learn at your own pace and eliminates any excuses. If you put in the effort, success is guaranteed!

📞 872-213-5858

✉️ publishernina@gmail.com

◎ @ninamotivates

🌐 www.ninaaddison.com

Additional Resources

Honeybook.com for contracts, invoices, appointments etc.

Placeit.com for book mockups.

www.fiverr.com for covers, editing, flyers, formatting, and so much more!

Chatgpt.com for tips and recommendations of writing prompts etc.

https://www.grammarly.com to spell check and edit your book.

https://www.goodreads.com to promote your book.

https://www.ilovepdf.com/ Free PDF creator website

To receive payments

www.squareup.com

https://www.payoneer.com/

https://stripe.com/

https://payhip.com/

https://www.shopify.com/

www.etsy.com

How to ship your books

You can get free shipping boxes from USPS. You could also get bubble envelopes or boxes from Amazon or your local stores. If your book is a 6x9, get an 8x10 envelope or bigger. When you ship from USPS, ship "media mail" which is the most affordable shipping cost. I usually send my customers an email or text afterwards letting them know their book has been shipped and provide the tracking number.

Get professional headshots done! Or use those wonderful phones but make them look professional. There's an app for that!

Create an email just for book business.

Get a google number. This is free and optional. You do not want your personal number in cyber space.

Order one copy of your book before you order a bulk of your books! This is to ensure you have caught every mistake or correction you want to make before you print and ship your books out.

The Book Launch

Celebrate your achievement! While the book is in the editing phase, you have time to plan, promote, and sell. You deserve a book launch. You can do this virtually or in-person. Find a local bookstore, coffee shop, or even the library. Or your local church. Do not go for broke for your book launch! Spend less and earn more. Give supporters a gift in the form of a bookmark or something small.

Ghost Writing

Many people want to write a book without writing a book. They want to tell their story to someone and have them bring it to life. If this is you, know that this is perfectly normal. There are many people who use ghost writers and many people who ghost write.

You want a writer experienced in your genre. Someone who can capture your voice and ideas accurately. The book should still sound like you. Discuss their process and turnaround time. You will need to meet with them and give them time to transcribe your writing. Know your vision and goals. Trust the process!

BONUS – Starting A Publishing Company

The first part is knowing how to publish a book! Congratulations on following this book and first publishing your own book! Now you absolutely can do it for others. I recommend getting a test client who will allow you to publish for them. Give them a deal. When I first started, I undercharged because I did not have all this information. You must consider all you will have to pay for. Everything you did for yourself you will have to do for your client. You want a contract listing all you will give them. You want this to protect yourself, and so your client knows what to expect.

Know what you are willing to do and not do. If there is a certain genre of books you are not willing to publish, make sure your clients know that. Everyone is not your client.

There are some legal things you want to get in place. Choose a business name. Make it make sense. Make it easy for people to know what you do. Then incorporate through your secretary of state. Get an EIN for free through the IRS website. Open a bank account. Get a website.

You can host workshops, do reels/shorts, make posts etc. to get people to see who you are and what you do. Building credibility will be very important.

You also do not have to nor want to do it alone. Build a team. You want editors, graphic designers, PR and Marketing team, illustrators, and know what printing distributors you will use. Even if you have one of each person on your team. You also want to have agreements with your team. What do they charge and how will you pay them. This should be included in your fee. Then you also need to know how much you want to make. There are people who format, or you can format yourself.

It is your turn to write!